Georgia Law requires Library materials to
be returned or replacement
Failure to comply is a mis
punishable by law. (O.C.G

17.95

D1036811

WITHDRAWN

St. Marys Public Library
100 Herb Bauer Drive
St. Marys, GA 31558

ST. MARYS PUBLIC LIBRARY

CARETAKERS
OF THE EARTH

Kathlyn Gay

ENSLOW PUBLISHERS, INC.

Bloy St. & Ramsey Ave.   P.O. Box 38
Box 777   Aldershot
Hillside, NJ 07205   Hants GU12 6BP
U.S.A.   U.K.

J-363.7
G
99003034

Copyright © 1993 by Kathlyn Gay

All rights reserved.

No part of this book may be reproduced by any means
without the written permission of the publisher.

Library of Congress Cataloging-In-Publication Data
Gay, Kathlyn.
Caretakers of the earth/Kathlyn Gay.
p. cm
Includes bibliographical references and index.
Summary: Describes various ways both individuals and groups can
get involved in helping protect the environment both locally and
globally.
ISBN 0-89490-397-7
1. Environmental protection—United States—Citizen participation—
Juvenile literature. 2. Environmental protection—Citizen
participation—Juvenile literature. I. Title.
TD171.7.G46   1993
363.7'0525—dc20   92-23048
                                                         CIP
                                                          AC

Printed in the United State of America

10 9 8 7 6 5 4 3 2 1

Illustration Credits:

California Energy Commission, p. 79; Center for Marine Conservation,
pp. 42, 44; Citizen's Clearinghouse for Hazardous Waste, p. 68; City of
Portland, Bureau of Environmental Services, p. 49; City Volunteer
Corps of NYC, p. 22; Connecticut Dept. of Environmental Protection,
p. 59; Crippled Children's Hospital and School in Sioux Falls, South
Dakota and teacher Leanne Baldwin. p. 61; Kathlyn Gay, pp. 7, 11,
28, 31, 36, 46, 54, 56, 73, 76, 83, 85; USDA, Agricultural Research
Service, p. 14; U.S. Geological Survey, Photo by Daniel C. Hahl, p.
19; The Wilderness Society, Photo by Janet Fries, p. 9; WE CAN, p.
64.

Cover Photo: Cover photo courtesy of the Student Conservation
Association, which provides outdoor volunteer opportunities in national
parks and wilderness areas nationwide.

ST. MARYS PUBLIC LIBRARY

Contents

1
Who Cares?

"Earth Day Every Day."

"Make a Difference."

"Plant a Tree, Cool the Globe."

"Protect the Rain Forests."

"Save the Dolphins."

"Stop Marine Debris."

"Conserve Energy."

Who hasn't heard or read the many environmental slogans bandied about today? Slogans help call attention to environmental problems that threaten our immediate environment as well as the global commons, the earth that is home for all living things. But it takes more than slogans to protect the planet. It takes many helping hands and energy, time, and money. Fortunately, people across the

United States, and around the world for that matter, are turning their concern for the environment into action.

Early Caretakers

The earliest caretakers of the environment in the Americas were the indigenous people—those native to the land. Tribal groups who first inhabited the continent were well aware that all of life on earth is interconnected. In fact, Native American culture is based on the idea of protecting Mother Earth. But most European colonists, unlike indigenous Americans, believed they had to tame nature. They feared the wilderness and were convinced it was infested with wild beasts and savages.

For two centuries, settlers pressed across the continent, cutting down forests, plowing up land, damming rivers, constructing roads, laying rail lines, building cities, and industrializing the nation. For the most part, people did not question the wisdom of taming the land. Changing the environment to suit humans was called development and was thought to be a sign of progress.

Yet there were nature lovers of all kinds in the late 1800s who called for the conservation of America's natural resources. What is conservation? In general, it means protecting land (soil), water, forests, and minerals and making wise use of these limited and sometimes nonrenewable resources. It also means protecting wildlife from extinction. Many species of birds, animals, plants, and marine life no longer exist because of urban growth.

Native American powwows, held in many areas of North America, include dances that celebrate the bounty of Mother Earth.

In spite of great opposition from industrialists, miners, ranchers, and others who believed that natural resources should be available for commercial use whenever needed, conservationists led the way to passage of some protective laws. They helped convince the U.S. Congress to enact legislation that set aside land for national parks, national forests, and wilderness preserves.

During the more recent past, the public became aware of other threats to the environment. Manufacturing, agriculture, transportation, and many human activities contributed to pollution of air, land, and water. People could see that rivers and lakes were choked with debris and contaminants. Smoke and smog darkened many big cities.

Earth Day Calls for Action

One of the first major events to call for citizen and government action to deal with pollution problems in the United States was the Earth Day celebration held in 1970. Gaylord Nelson, who was then a U.S. senator, came up with the idea and helped set up the event. Earth Day sparked many volunteer efforts to clean up the environment and prompted groups to press for protective legislation. "Once the public spoke out, the legislators began to move," Nelson said.[1]

During the 1970s, the U.S. Congress passed many landmark bills to protect the environment, including the Clean Water Act, the Clean Air Act, and the Toxic

Gaylord Nelson, founder of the first Earth Day in 1970, is a former U. S. senator from Wisconsin. In the Senate, he sponsored numerous bills to protect America's natural resources.

Substances Control Act. And state legislators passed environmental protection laws, too.

States and cities made some progress in cleaning up foul air and water. But by 1990, the twentieth anniversary celebrations of Earth Day still focused on the serious threats to the environment—some more serious than the concerns of two decades before. Problems like global warming and depletion of the ozone layer affect not just Americans but people around the world as well.

In spite of some victories, there are huge battles ahead, according to Denis Hayes, who helped launch the first Earth Day event and coordinated the 1990 celebration. Hayes often points out that people tend to believe science and technology will bring about the necessary changes needed to protect the environment. But, in fact, he emphasizes that we all need to be part of efforts to care for the earth.

Indeed, people from all walks of life are beginning to realize they can do something to reduce or eliminate the use of materials that pollute and to conserve nonrenewable natural resources. Some earth advocates and protectors are well known and have received awards for their efforts. A few have taken great risks, even losing their lives, in campaigns to restore or protect a natural habitat or to alert citizens about pollutants that endanger their health. But most environmental activists are recognized only in their local communities or neighborhoods. Their concerns have led them to take responsibility for sustaining and nurturing the part of the earth that sustains and nurtures them.

Reusing containers, such as a plastic jug to buy spring water, is just one simple way to be a "green" consumer.

2
Today's Conservationists

Today, thousands of volunteers are at work around the globe trying to conserve our natural resources. Some work on international projects such as campaigns to set aside the Antarctic continent as a "World Park" or wilderness area. The designation would help protect it.

Conservationists also take part in missions to save tropical rain forests, risking their lives and being jailed for their opposition to mass destruction of trees and ecosystems. Or they attempt to preserve seacoasts and offshore ocean waters from oil drilling or other activities, such as urban construction, that can damage ecosystems. Volunteers restore natural habitats—land, waterways, and seashores—that have been polluted or damaged.

In recent years, international organizations have honored individuals and groups for their preservation work, offering awards such as the "Earth Prize" that was created by Claes Nobel, greatgrandnephew of the Alfred Nobel who originated the well-known Nobel Prizes. The United Nations Environment Programme presents a number of awards for adults and youth who have made significant contributions to environmental preservation.

The Goldman Foundation, set up by Richard and Rhoda Goldman, a wealthy couple in San Francisco, presents six awards annually, for one environmental hero or heroine on each continent. The Goldmans, who have been nature lovers all their lives, awarded the first six prizes of $60,000 each during Earth Day ceremonies in April 1990. The prizes were designed to recognize "the grassroots heroes of the world, people who have taken great risks . . . to save the world's environment," Richard Goldman said.[1] Usually, the prizes have been used to continue environmental projects or to repay individuals for their financial sacrifices and long-term efforts.

Working in Their Own Backyards

Many environmental projects are worldwide or national in scope. But people working on their own land or in their own communities carry out some of the most effective conservation and restoration efforts.

Numerous farmers, for example, are now conserving or restoring the topsoil on their lands. Across the United States, intensive farming methods have been reducing topsoil. In order to grow acres and acres of a few major

A researcher with the U.S. Department of Agriculture compares a normal hornworm, a crop pest, with a stunted worm. Along with other scientists, he is studying ways to destroy pests without using chemical pesticides that can contaminate soil and groundwater.

crops, most farmers over the past few decades have been using large amounts of chemical pesticides and fertilizers. The chemicals have destroyed some of the living organisms needed to make soil healthy. When this happens, the soil degrades and becomes dry and loose and then blows away or erodes with water runoff.

To conserve the topsoil, about 5 percent of U.S. farmers and about 1 percent of Canadian farmers have turned to sustainable agricultural methods. These growers have reduced or eliminated the use of chemical pesticides and fertilizers. They plant crops that add nutrients to the soil and practice crop rotation, planting a different crop in a field each season or every second or third season, which helps enrich the soil. Planting trees and shrubs along fields is another way farmers protect their land from wind and water erosion.[2]

In many communities, individual volunteers and citizen groups work to restore or preserve natural areas, whether they are tallgrass prairies, ravines, creeks, woodlands, shorelines, or nature trails in state and national parks. Frequently chapters of such organizations as the Nature Conservancy, the Sierra Club, the Audubon Society, the Izaak Walton League of America, and the Wilderness Society carry out the work.

Government agencies also are responsible for conservation. State departments of natural resources, fish and wildlife services, and soil conservation agencies are examples. Some projects are conducted by young people who

Did You Know That . . .

- About 25 percent of all bottles manufactured in the United States are made from recycled glass.

- A TV set will run for three hours on the amount of energy saved by recycling an aluminum can.

- Recycling a ton of waste paper saves 3,700 pounds of lumber and 24,000 gallons of water.

- Oregon was the first state to pass a "bottle bill," a law requiring deposits on beverage bottles and cans so that the containers would be returned to stores for recycling.

- About 27 percent of the 240 million tires thrown away each year in the United States are recapped or recycled into new rubber products.

- The National Wildlife Federation estimates that printing its 1990 catalog of educational materials on recycled paper saved 275 trees, conserved over 100,000 gallons of water and 65,000 kilowatt hours of energy, and kept 1,000 pounds of air pollutants out of the atmosphere.

- The city of Osage, Iowa, is known as the "Conservation Capital of the Nation" because its energy conservation program has saved the 3,800 residents an estimated $1.2 million each year in energy costs.

- More than 2,144 miles of footpath within a protective corridor of backcountry wilderness, stretching from Maine to northern Georgia, has been preserved with the help of 4,600 volunteers who work year-round on conservation projects.

- At least 1,000 communities across the United States conduct hazardous waste collection programs.

- The total number of environmental groups increased from about 200 in 1975 to more than 350 in 1990; membership increased sixfold during the period, from 2 million to 12 million.

- American, Soviet, and Chinese climbers scaled Mount Everest in 1989 and cleaned up 4,000 pounds of trash left over the years by previous climbers.

- The U.S. Code of Federal Regulations on protecting the environment contains over 11,000 pages.

- A *USA Weekend* magazine survey of 11,000 readers in 1991 found that since Earth Day 1990, 86 percent of the respondents had made lifestyle changes to care for the earth.

Sources: World Wildlife Fund, the National Wildlife Federation, the Chemical Manufacturers Association, U.S. Council on Environmental Quality, and *USA Weekend*

are part of a state Conservation Corps or Youth Corps. Members of the Student Conservation Association, for example, have restored trails and bridges in Yellowstone Park and also have restored sections of the park damaged by fire-fighting activities a few years ago.

A variety of individual and community projects are helping protect marshes, swamps, and bogs—collectively called wetlands. For centuries people worldwide have thought of marshes and swamps as wastelands, and many have been drained, filled in, or damaged by pollutants. Since the 1600s, more than half of the original 200 million acres of wetlands in the United States have been destroyed.[3]

During recent years, however, environmental groups and U.S. government agencies have been calling attention to the benefits of wetlands. These habitats serve as filters for surface runoffs of water and sometimes hold overflow of water from streams and rivers, preventing flooding. Many wetlands are spawning sites for fish and homes for a great variety of birds and wildlife.

Along the Platte River near Grand Island, Nebraska, are wetlands and flats where an estimated 500,000 sandhill cranes come each spring. The birds rest, feed, and mate before they continue their migration from the south to their summer homes in Canada and Alaska. Craig Fannes, a biologist with the U.S. Fish and Wildlife Service, has been able to show the value of these habitats to students. He takes them on field trips to visit the wetlands along the Platte River. An avid bird watcher, Fannes is considered a

Researchers with the U.S. Geological Survey take samples from rivers and other waterways to determine whether the water is polluted.

hero to young people in the Grand Island area because of his work to preserve the cranes' habitat.

For years the area has been threatened by plans to build two dams in order to provide water for suburbs many miles upstream in the growing metropolitan area of Denver, Colorado. The dams would cut off the flow of water, which already has diminished, and would destroy all types of wildlife along the river's course, biologists say. In late 1990, the U.S. Environmental Protection Agency (EPA) refused to issue permits for the dams. William K. Reilly, EPA administrator, said there would be "significant loss and damage" to not only miles of wetlands but also trout fishing and other recreation areas on the river.[4]

One effort that has called attention to the need to preserve the area has been an annual three-day event called "Wings Over the Platte," which Craig Fannes helped develop. The spring event celebrates the migration of sandhill cranes. People come from around the world to see the mighty birds, which stand about three-and-one-half feet tall and have a wing span of five feet. More public understanding of the need to protect the birds' habitat is crucial to saving it. Many environmentalists believe that the conflict over preserving the site is almost symbolic. It represents the many disputes over the years that have occurred and will continue to occur between conservationists and developers.

Teenage Activists

Young people also are preservationists, fighting to protect or restore natural habitats in their own communities or backyards or urban neighborhoods. For example, the New York City Volunteer Corps (CVC) members, who range in age from seventeen to twenty, take part in a number of efforts to improve the urban environment. The New York CVC is one of numerous volunteer service programs in cities across the United States from Boston to Los Angeles. The National Community Service Commission established by the U.S. Congress in 1990 funds such programs.

In New York, CVC members provide full-time volunteer services for over 300 projects in exchange for work experience, education, and training. After a year of service, volunteers choose between a $5,000 scholarship or a $2,500 cash grant. The projects include a variety of services from tutoring young children to helping the elderly. But many efforts focus on the environment. Volunteers convert vacant lots into thriving gardens of flowers and vegetables, plant trees in neighborhoods, clean up beaches, and improve city parks. "In 1991, CVC provided the Department of Parks and Recreation with over 36,000 hours of service on over 70 projects," says Diana Echeverria, public affairs officer for CVC.[5]

After a six-year campaign, students in Lee County, on the Gulf Coast of southern Florida, have been able to save a cypress swamp that would have been drained and filled in for urban development. The teenagers are part of a

Members of the City Volunteer Corps clear away a hillside in Morningside Park in New York City. The corps also works on soil erosion and other environmental projects for the city's park department.

long-standing educational project known as the Monday Group, initiated by William Hammond, the director of Lee County's environmental education services.

To develop their leadership skills, students from junior and senior high schools in the county take part every Monday in a variety of environmental projects. In their campaign to save the swamp, the students wrote and sent out news stories about the project. They talked with county officials and citizen groups. Their efforts helped convince voters to pass a referendum that provided for $2.5 million in tax funds to buy the swampland.[6]

A small creek that needed restoration caught the attention of a young environmentalist in Portland, Oregon. Twelve-year-old Hugh Farrish started his project at the end of the 1990–91 school year. He found that development in the area had affected the creek. Silt had collected in the stream, changing its meandering course to a rushing channel that supported little wildlife. Farrish wanted to bring back frogs and trout.

After studying books on fish habitat, Farrish enlisted the help of his younger brother and built stone gates in the stream, trying to slow the water's flow. But he needed additional advice, so he contacted a biologist at the Oregon Department of Fish and Wildlife who worked with him on a restoration plan.

With the help of his neighbors, Farrish carefully stacked and anchored several dozen dried-up Christmas trees along the stream to create pools for fish. The pools are expected to attract insects first, then frogs, and within a couple of years trout should swim up from a larger creek and feed on the food supply available in the restored creek.

Another young conservationist is Andrew Holleman, age sixteen, of Chelmsford, Massachusetts. When he was twelve years old, he learned that a developer was planning to build a condominium complex on lush wooded land that is half wetland. The site is near Andrew's home and is a special place to him and his family. The Hollemans have spent many hours enjoying the birds, wood turtles, plants, and other wildlife in the area.

In an article about his experiences, published in *Mother Earth News*, Holleman explained that he learned Massachusetts law protects wetlands and that only a portion of the site was suitable for development. So he wrote a petition, got registered voters among his neighbors to sign it, and explained how building the condominium could destroy the woods. He also requested advice from a biologist at the Massachusetts Audubon Society, who instructed him to continue his efforts to rally local support.

Over nearly a year's time, people gathered for many town meetings, and a neighborhood association was formed. Holleman and his neighbors raised almost $16,000 to pay the costs of legal fees and research by an environmental scientist. Finally, tests showed the wooded wetland was not suitable for the type of complex the developer planned, and the town of Chelmsford denied the permit needed to build the condominium.

For now, the land is safe, but Holleman is attempting to get the state or city to buy the property so that it will be permanently protected. But so far, there are not enough funds available, and Holleman has applied for financial help from the Nature Conservancy and other organizations. Part of the mission of the Nature Conservancy is to purchase land from private owners and set it aside as preserves. In this manner, the organization has been able to save millions of acres across the United States and in other countries.

In his magazine article, Holleman noted that people often get discouraged and think they "can't fight city hall" when trying to protect the environment. But he challenged readers not to give up. "If you believe in something, you have to stand up for it. Don't ever give up the fight against a poorly sited development, pollution, or anything environmentally dangerous. If you do, you are giving up on the world. Even if you don't win, at least you will have tried."[7]

3
Protecting Forests and Planting Trees

Countless writers and speakers in recent years have described the benefits of woodlands and forests. Although most people are aware of the value of trees for such purposes as fuel, building materials, and paper-making (from wood pulp), perhaps there has never been a time when trees seemed more important as environmental saviors. They keep soil from eroding, hold moisture in the ground, and provide homes for birds and diverse animals. Trees frequently serve as filters for air pollutants and help cut energy consumption because they protect buildings from the hot sun and cold winds. Trees also are "sinks," or holding places, for carbon dioxide, a trace gas that is essential for life.

With all the advantages that trees provide, it would seem reasonable to conserve them and use them wisely. But consumers worldwide demand many types of wood products and construction materials. As a result, people who want to preserve trees frequently are in conflict with people who want to cut them down. These conflicts have become heated and sometimes violent in temperate forest regions in the United States and Canada and in tropical rain-forest regions of the world.

Ancient Forests

In the United States, the controversy rages over the fast-dwindling ancient forests, also known as "old-growth forests," located in the Pacific Northwest. Most lumber companies cut timber from privately owned woodlands, but national forests are the source of 20 percent of the nation's timber. Some of these national forests contain old-growth trees.

Because of an economic recession during the 1980s, logging companies in the Northwest were unable to pay high costs for timber. To spur the sagging economy in the region, lawmakers pressured the U.S. Forest Service to increase the amount of low-cost timber sold each year from national forests. Since then lumber companies have been allowed to harvest 400,000 acres of forest land annually. They use a practice called clear-cutting, stripping sections of forest of all trees in a relatively short span of time.

Although seedlings are planted to replace the cut trees, many biologists are concerned because a diverse and complex ecosystem is replaced with just a few species of trees.

A section of forest in the Pacific Northwest has been clear-cut, stripped of trees. Biologists condemn the practice since it often leads to soil erosion that pollutes streams.

As a result, the trees are vulnerable to damage from insects and disease. Roads built to logging sites and the clear-cutting practice also lead to soil erosion and pollute streams.

Because of the demand for timber, only 10 percent of the original forest land in the Pacific Northwest region remains. Half of that could be cleared within the next fifty years if present practices continue.[1]

Protecting Forest Resources

The forests contain more than timber resources. They also are the habitat of a number of endangered species, one of which is the spotted owl. The spotted owl has gained the focus of attention because it is under the protection of federal conservation laws. But no laws protect endangered forests, so those wanting to save old-growth ecosystems must rely on laws that protect endangered species.

Spotted owls need old trees and space for survival. If the owls die off, that is a warning that the ecosystem is being destroyed, too. The number of owls has dropped by 50 percent since the mid-1900s. But people like Jim Farrell with the U.S. Forest Service in Oregon are studying the spotted owl, looking for signs that the species is still reproducing and hoping to alert the public to the need to save the owl's habitat.

Yet there are formidable obstacles. Fearing their jobs will be lost, loggers lash out at scientists and environmental groups working to save the forest for spotted owls. "Kill an

Owl, Save a Logger" is a slogan often used in timber country.[2]

Valuable yew trees also are found in ancient forests. About ten years ago, researchers discovered that the bark of ancient Pacific yew trees in the old-growth forests produces a chemical called taxol, which is effective in treating some kinds of cancer. It is possible that other trees in the ancient forest also could provide life-saving medicines.

In 1990 the U.S. Forest Service revised its policies and reduced logging in national forests. Lumber company owners and employees protested, saying the economy of the forest region would suffer. They also predicted higher prices for wood products and building materials. Conservationists, on the other hand, believe there will be only slight increases in the price of lumber. In their opinion, the higher price would be worthwhile if an endangered ecosystem is saved.

Environmental groups continue to fight for preservation of the forests in the U.S. Northwest and also on Vancouver Island in British Columbia, Canada, where entire mountainsides have been scalped of trees. In Canada logging practices are not regulated as they are in the United States. Some Canadian foresters believe that old forests in British Columbia will be gone by the year 2060. The effects of logging also have caused landslides and destroyed much of the commercial salmon fishing along the coast.

Logs are piled up for shipment from the Pacific Northwest to many parts of the world. Conservationists believe national forests have been overcut, and they often criticize logging operations that destroy habitats for endangered animals.

To call attention to the need to preserve endangered ecosystems and national forests in both the United States and Canada, some activists have chained themselves to trees. Others have set up blockades along logging roads to prevent loggers from getting to cutting sites. In British Columbia a group of teenagers occupied the office of the Minister of Forests in Victoria, the capital of the province. The young people staged a hunger strike to try to halt further logging on Vancouver Island.

Many environmentalists, however, work in less confrontational ways. Citizens in states as diverse as Arkansas, North Carolina, Oregon, and Montana have organized watchdog groups to alert the public to poor management practices in forests. These groups foster community action campaigns to stop clear-cutting practices. They pressure legislators to enact protective laws or make provisions to enforce laws designed to preserve national forests. Some activists monitor water quality of forest streams and try to halt the use of toxic herbicides (weed killers) dangerous to wildlife in wooded areas.

Saving Tropical Rain Forests

In tropical regions, many of which are in developing nations, governments encourage forest clearing because lumbering provides income from export products. In Latin American nations, for example, forests have been cleared not only to produce lumber but also to provide grazing land to raise cattle. The cattle provide inexpensive beef products demanded by consumers in North America.

With rapidly increasing populations in developing nations, people must cut down trees for fuel and clear forests to plant crops. Yet in many poor nations, the cleared land is not suitable for long-term farming. The soil soon loses its nutrients and erodes, so people must move on to clear even more forest land. In earlier times, people could move back to a land area in a few years when the soil had recovered. But such a farming system breaks down when there are increases in population and demands for land to cultivate.

An estimated fifty to one hundred acres of tropical forests are cleared each minute.[3] This rapid destruction leads to numerous problems. Indigenous people—those whose ancestors lived in the forests for thousands of years—depend on the forest ecosystem for their survival and way of life. When native people are forced to leave the land, they frequently must move to urban areas where they find only low-paying jobs and are exposed to diseases they have never known before. The stress of these life changes also leads to serious health hazards and even death.

Deforestation destroys many plants that are used to make a variety of medicines, such as painkillers and prescription drugs for heart disease and cancer. Tropical forests also contain many more species of wildlife and plants than are in the ancient forests of the Pacific Northwest. Many species cannot be found anywhere else in the world and for the most part have not been studied or classified.

Another major problem related to deforestation is the release of carbon dioxide from trees that are cut or burned. Carbon dioxide and other trace gases from fossil fuel burning have been building up in the atmosphere, contributing to the greenhouse effect, or global warming. Most atmospheric scientists believe the greenhouse effect will lead to climate changes that cause flooding in low-lying coastal regions and affect food production around the world.

Because of the problems associated with deforestation, many environmental groups and government leaders are trying to find ways to preserve areas of tropical forests. In some cases, environmental organizations like the Nature Conservancy have been able to swap forest land for debt. The organization buys a section of forest from the government of a developing nation and sets the land aside for a preserve. Funds from the land sales are used to pay off some of the debt the tropical country owes to the United States or other affluent countries. To support debt-for-nature swaps, local groups, including youth groups, across North America and in other nations conduct fund-raising events.

The Rainforest Action Network (RAN), based in San Francisco, is promoting another approach. It is calling for consumers to boycott wood products from tropical forests as a way to protest deforestation. Some lawmakers in the United States are considering bans on the use of tropical timber, and in a few European countries, local governments already prohibit the use of tropical timber for public building projects.

But the Rainforest Alliance of New York City points out that more than timber is at stake. Bananas, coffee, and cocoa (chocolate) are other products from tropical forests. It would be difficult to convince a large number of American consumers to do without these favorites. Thus the Rainforest Alliance has launched a program called Smart Wood, which is a kind of "reverse boycott," according to the alliance's news bureau.

The Smart Wood program offers positive incentives by certifying companies that harvest tropical woods in socially and environmentally responsible ways. To earn the certification, companies have to meet certain standards, such as protecting local people from the adverse effects of logging and managing forests so that they can be sustained rather than completely destroyed.[4]

Planting Trees

While national and international leaders confront the global issues of forest destruction, people around the world have been planting trees. No one claims this is a global solution to problems associated with deforestation, but certainly it is an effective way for individuals to do their part to care for the earth. In many developing nations, for example, people plant food-bearing trees, adding to the food supply, stemming soil erosion, and providing shade.

Tree-planting projects are carried out by many student groups across the United States.

During the late 1970s, Wangari Maathal, a professor at the University of Nairobi, Kenya, founded what has become a successful Green Belt Movement in Africa. The program is operated primarily by women, and its goal is to reclaim desert areas that continue to expand because trees have been cleared from the land. Ten million trees have been planted under the program, which has spread to other African nations. Maathal received a Goldman award in 1991 for her heroic efforts.[5]

In the United States, tree planting is, of course, the focus of Arbor Day celebrations (arbor is the Latin word for tree). More than a century ago, Julius Morton came up with the idea for a national arbor day after moving from the East coast to Nebraska where there were few trees. Morton inspired German immigrants living on the prairies to plant trees, especially orchards. Later he founded the National Arbor Day Foundation, which today sponsors a Trees for America Campaign and Tree City USA, a program to encourage tree-planting in U.S. urban areas.

Another major tree-planting effort has been under way in California for more than twenty years. Called TreePeople, it began during the 1970s with Andy Lipkis, then age 15, who was concerned about dying trees in the Los Angeles National Forest. Exhausts from motor vehicles and the resulting smog created stress on trees, eventually killing them. Lipkis and his wife, Katie, are now the motivating forces behind a program that has encouraged volunteers to plant over two million trees in Los Angeles. TreePeople has sparked similar efforts in nations around the world.

In 1989 the Global ReLeaf program of the American Forestry Association began a national campaign to plant 100 million new trees in towns and cities across the United States. Planting trees around buildings can reduce the need for energy. This, in turn, cuts the amount of carbon dioxide released from energy-producing sources. Growing trees also absorb carbon dioxide. Every ton of new wood grown removes about 1.47 tons of carbon dioxide from the air, according to Global ReLeaf reports.

Numerous stories about tree-planting projects appear in Global ReLeaf newsletters and other published materials and in many major newspapers and magazines. One example is a Trees for Tucson-Global ReLeaf program in which volunteers plant trees that adapt to the Arizona desert climate. A number of community groups cooperate in the project, and they expect to plant 500,000 trees by 1996.

Young people in New Mexico bring together a cross section of citizens in Tree New Mexico Programs in which volunteers will plant 16 million trees by 2000. Trees for Mother Earth in Colorado is a major environmental program of the Navajo nation; the focus is planting fruit trees on Navajo reservations. Volunteers with California's Nature Conservancy plant and maintain trees along waterways and have replaced vegetation on more than 200 acres.

Many tree-planting projects are the work of 4-H groups, Sierra Clubs, Keep America Beautiful programs, the Wilderness Society, the National Audubon Society, the Nature Conservancy, urban forestry programs, and other organizations. Tree-planting programs also begin because student groups, families or individual citizens realize tree planting is a relatively simple way to take positive action right in their own yards or neighborhoods.

Conrad Kramer in northern Indiana began the Living Earth Reforestation program in 1991 because he wanted to do more than contribute to organizations protecting tropical rain forests and old-growth forests in the Pacific Northwest. He believed that areas near his home should be reforested. Kramer organized a project to plant seedlings—oaks, pines, and other types suitable for the climate and soil—on sites along a new highway where denuded land needed erosion control. The group plans to continue such efforts in the years ahead.

With a little guidance just about anyone can plant tree seedlings and nurture them so they will grow. You can get advice on how to plant a tree from a local nursery or from the Global ReLeaf program, the Arbor Day Foundation, or some of the other organizations listed in the Where to Write section. By planting a tree, you not only help the environment. You also plant a symbol that says you care about the future and the planet that the next generation will inherit.

4
Saving Water Resources

Our lives and those of other creatures on earth depend on safe water supplies. But parts of the oceans and some seas, lakes, rivers, streams, creeks, and groundwater have been polluted. Waste and debris from industry, agriculture, logging, mining, and many other types of human activities contaminate water, endangering aquatic life and wildlife on land and threatening human health.

The need to clean up water resources is urgent in most of the industrialized world, including North America. Fortunately, people are responding in a variety of ways that range from clearing rubbish from rivers and seacoasts to complex efforts to prevent toxic chemicals from polluting groundwater supplies.

Efforts to Stop Marine Debris

Although an international law bans dumping plastics and most hazardous wastes at sea, people still dump trash in ocean waters. Garbage and other debris then washes ashore. "Marine debris knows no geographic boundaries. Litter dumped overboard in the Pacific can find its way to Japan or California. The problem must be addressed through international efforts," declares the Center for Marine Conservation (CMC).[1]

Those efforts include Citizen Pollution Patrols sponsored by CMC. The groups clean up beaches in the spring and fall along the coasts of the United States and its territories and the coasts of Canada, Mexico, Guatemala, Japan, and Taiwan. More than 105,000 volunteers participated in these events during 1990.

Along with collecting trash, volunteers catalog the types of debris and identify the sources of some of the trash. Commercial and recreational fishing boats, for example, are the sources of items like plastic rope and plastic fishing lines. Volunteers cleaning up U.S. coastal areas also have been able to identify trash from cruise ships and debris from more than fifty countries.

Yet land sources account for much more of the debris in oceans. Rivers and streams carry throwaways to the sea. Sewage discharges, beach and dock litter, and industrial discharges into waterways also contribute to ocean debris and pollution on shore.

More than 100,000 volunteers took part in beach cleanups during 1990.

Part of the trash collected on beaches has been recycled. On the East Coast, for example, 6,000 volunteers took part in a 1990 "Clean the Bay Day" along the Chesapeake. Volunteers sorted the trash, setting aside plastic materials for recycling at Trimax Plastic Lumber in Long Island, New York. The company manufactured park benches from the plastic and donated them to each cleanup location.[2]

Saving Marine Life

Plastic debris, which can last for hundreds of years, is a major environmental problem in the water as well as on shore. Plastics endanger aquatic life in oceans, lakes, and streams. Within the past few years, news stories and TV documentaries have called attention to fish, mammals, and birds that have been strangled by plastic six-pack rings or have been entangled in fishing nets. Wildlife frequently mistake plastic for food and may be poisoned by it. Plastic also fills the stomach. As a result, animals and birds do not eat and die of starvation.

Dozens of environmental organizations have joined in efforts to publicize the marine debris hazard and to discourage dumping in water bodies and streams. Along with spreading information about marine debris, organizations also have alerted the public to a related issue: dolphin deaths. The United Nations estimates that each year as many as 100,000 dolphins are killed when caught in

Six-pack rings, fishing nets and other debris can endanger wildlife such as this seal. Thousands of birds and mammals die due to entanglement with plastic debris such as this each year.

mile-long driftnets used in tuna fishing. It is the largest destruction of marine mammals on earth.[3]

The Humane Society has long protested the slaughter of dolphins. But it was not until the latter part of 1989 that Americans across the land became incensed over the needless killing. Individuals and groups organized boycotts against tuna companies that destroyed dolphins in tuna driftnets. Student groups protested the use of tuna in school lunches. And many other groups studied the lives of dolphins, sharing their information about these intelligent mammals and the need to protect them.

Only about 10 percent of the tuna sold in the United States is caught in driftnets that also capture dolphins. But until recently customers had no way of knowing how tuna was caught and whether dolphins were endangered in the process. The boycotts and public information programs helped spur the tuna industry to label tuna that is "dolphin safe." Star Kist Seafood Company was the first to announce in April 1990 that the company would use only tuna caught by methods that do not destroy dolphins. In June 1991, the company was awarded a U.N. Global 500 award, which is given for outstanding efforts to protect and improve the environment.[4]

Other projects have helped save aquatic life. One example is the ongoing program of the California Marine Mammal Center that is staffed by a few professionals and over 400 volunteers. The volunteers help rescue and rehabilitate sick or injured marine mammals, eventually

The Star Kist Seafood Company places a "dolphin safe" label on its cans of tuna. Several other tuna companies use a similar label to indicate that their tuna fishing does not endanger dolphins.

returning the animals to their natural habitat. A volunteer Sea Turtle Beach Patrol in Florida records information about sea turtle activities so that conservationists can protect the endangered turtles. (Thousands of sea turtles are caught and killed in nets used to catch shrimp.) And many citizen groups have helped recover and clean up sea animals and birds that have been covered with oil after tanker accidents or spills from oil drilling off North American coasts.

Monitoring and Preserving Rivers and Streams

The quality of some streams and rivers is so poor in many parts of the world that these waterways have been labeled "chemical sewers." In most cases, there are multiple sources of pollution. Before attempts can be made to clean up waterways, pollutants and their sources must be identified. Volunteer groups often help with this process.

Sometimes the efforts start with a concerned individual like Bob Parent of Scituate, Massachusetts. Parent became increasingly upset when clam beds in the North River marshes declined year after year. Clams not only decreased in size and number but also were considered unsafe to eat because of the polluted waters.

Parent and other citizens believed overflow from the local sewage treatment plant was the cause of the problem, but state officials disagree, saying ocean waters would wash pollutants out to sea. To help settle the dispute, a citizens' monitoring program called Adopt-a-Stream, under the state's Fish and Wildlife Department, began during the summer of 1990.

Once a month Adopt-a-Stream volunteers compile information about the river's fourteen tributaries. They fill out questionnaires about the color of the water and odors from the river as well as weather conditions. Volunteers also use testing kits to measure chemicals that could be harmful to shellfish and other aquatic life and determine the pH levels—the acidity—of the water. Such monitoring will provide a long-term record of the tributaries and pinpoint pollution sources.

Wherever there are damaged or polluted waterways today, there is a need for small or large group efforts to protect these resources. Save Our Streams is the largest U.S. network of trained volunteers who monitor and restore streams and rivers. These programs are a major emphasis of the Izaak Walton League of America and its chapters across the country.

Citizen monitoring and cleanup campaigns also are initiated by state and local agencies. In the Chesapeake Bay region, for example, various agencies in Maryland, Virginia, Pennsylvania, and the District of Columbia are part of a cooperative effort that is helping educate the public about ways to protect the bay.

In 1983 the EPA released a study showing that the bay had been seriously polluted because of urban development in the drainage basin—the area drained by rivers and

DUMP NO WASTE

DRAINS TO STREAM

Nationwide, many student volunteers paint stencils like this on curbs or on the street near storm drains. Stenciling programs remind people that drains are for rainwater only. Volunteers hope to discourage people from dumping chemicals, paints, pesticides, motor oil, and other hazardous material into drains. Waste materials dumped into drains go directly into streams or groundwater, contaminating these water sources.

streams that empty into the Chesapeake. More than 15 million people live along waterways of the basin. Numerous volunteer groups are now taking actions to protect the bay. These include projects to plant shrubs and trees on the banks of streams to prevent soil erosion, stream cleanups, and efforts to reduce the use of toxic chemicals that drain into waterways.

An award-winning monitoring program in a different part of the United States has been going on since 1988 at the University of Michigan School of Natural Resources. Called the Global River Environmental Education Network (GREEN), the program evolved from a local project. Professor William Stapp and students in the School of Natural Resources developed and carried out the original project. It was a successful "action research" campaign monitoring the Rouge River in southeastern Michigan—a heavily industrialized area. Students gained hands-on experience and were able to raise public awareness of water quality. They also set up a citizen's monitoring network and challenged urban development that threatened the river. The project evolved to become an outstanding resource for local monitoring programs across the United States and around the world.

GREEN members have traveled to U.S. schools and schools abroad to train elementary and secondary students in water monitoring procedures. GREEN also links people involved in water quality programs through newsletters and a computer network. In 1991 GREEN established an electronic conference on EcoNet, an international communications network that people in over fifty nations can access.

By sharing information, students, teachers, and many other citizens are able to effect changes that improve water quality. When participants learn that their actions are part of a global effort to improve water systems, they are empowered "to believe in themselves as vital stewards of the environment," one GREEN director noted.[5]

ST. MARYS PUBLIC LIBRARY

5
Wastebusters

"Reduce, reuse, recycle, recover."

You have probably heard or read those words many times. Every environmental organization, publication, and educational program about the environment has used the slogan at one time or another to stress solutions to the garbage crisis.

The problems associated with our throwaway society have been widely publicized. Solid waste—household garbage and trash and industrial wastes—have accumulated at municipal landfills, the sites where these materials are dumped. Most of the landfills across the United States are closing because there is no more room for solid waste or because they are unsafe.

Laws require that landfills be underlined with vinyl or clay materials or both. These materials trap leachate, the liquid from waste, at the bottom of the landfill. The leachate is drained off to prevent it from seeping through soil into groundwater, the source of drinking water for millions of Americans. In addition, layers of soil or vinyl must cover the trash so rain and snow melts do not seep through.

Because landfills are tightly compacted, many throwaway materials do not biodegrade, or break down, quickly. Bacteria in soil eat away at materials, but they need oxygen and water to work effectively. One of the main causes of the garbage crisis, then, is the fact that trash does not decompose quickly.

Packaging materials alone take up 30 percent of total landfill space in the United States. At the present rate of production, Americans will generate an estimated 62 million tons of throwaway packaging in the years ahead.[1]

The problem has an added dimension. Large amounts of raw materials and energy are needed to produce all the different types of packaging. Manufacturing bottles, cans, and other packaging depletes natural resources and creates environmental pollution—the very problems that the people described in previous chapters have been trying to solve.

How are Americans dealing with these related issues? Are they really reducing, reusing, recycling, and recovering materials? The answer appears to be yes, but much more could be done.

Although people have been recycling old newspapers and aluminum cans for decades, efforts have been slowly

The principal of an elementary school holds up a glass bottle to demonstrate the kinds of containers that students will be collecting for a recycling program.

increasing. Only about 10 percent of the solid waste generated in the United States was recycled in the 1980s, but that amount inched up to 14 percent in 1990, according to Winston Porter, a former EPA official and author of a recycling guide for schools. Porter believes that with growing awareness in schools and elsewhere of the need for recycling, nearly a third of the solid waste in the United States will be recycling by the year 2000. Still, that is much less than the goal set by a Canadian task force of packagers, consumer groups, and government officials. By 2005, Canada hopes to reduce its annual solid waste by 50 percent.[2]

Who is Recycling?

A great variety of waste reduction programs exist all across North America. Many Canadian and U.S. municipal governments have set up curbside recycling programs, which are voluntary or required by law. Citizens sort their recyclable materials—papers, glass, aluminum, and some plastics—and put them in specially marked bins for pick up at the curb. Some states have passed so-called bottle bills. These laws require that consumers pay a deposit on bottles and cans so that these containers will be returned for recycling.

An ever-increasing number of businesses also have started recycling efforts. Office workers, for example, collect used stationery, computer paper, copier paper, and plain envelopes for recycling. Such organizations as the

Students watch as the cans they have collected in a cleanup and recycling program travel up a conveyor. Magnets separate the steel cans from aluminum cans. Both types of cans are sent to smelters where they are melted down and reused to make new cans. Recycling efforts are not complete until throwaway items like these are reused as new products.

National Office Paper Recycling Project of the U.S. Conference of Mayors and the National Recycling Coalition can be of help for offices just starting a recycling effort.

In stores, warehouses, and industrial plants, a common recycling effort is to bale cardboard containers for sale to paper-making companies that will process the cardboard into recycled cardboard. Manufacturers that use metal materials usually send waste metals and aluminum to scrap-metal yards. The scrap is cut up or smashed and baled for shipment to smelters, where it is melted down for reuse in manufacturing plants. Processing scrap metals for reuse is one of the oldest recycling businesses in the world.

Farmers in a number of states are recycling old newspapers. They buy shredded newspaper from processors and use it for cattle bedding. The material absorbs waste from the livestock and is replaced every three days or so. Usually farmers use straw, corn cobs, and wood shavings as bedding, since these materials are available on the farm or are inexpensive to buy. But the idea of using newspapers is catching on. During the first three months of 1991, James Smoker of La Porte County, Indiana, bought more than 170 tons of newspaper from a city recycling program, paying only $3.00 per ton. Smoker shredded the paper himself and provided bedding material for 2,500 head of cattle.[3]

Groups ranging from the Audubon Society to the American Association of Retired People (AARP) to the League of Women Voters also are taking part in recycling efforts. During the twelve years that a northwestern Arkansas chapter of AARP has been collecting recyclable materials, the group has taken in 202,448 pounds of glass and 76,000 pounds of aluminum. The group also has collected 6 million pounds of paper—enough to fill a football field 10 feet deep.[4]

School Recyclers

Recyclers can be found in countless schools across North America. For example, students in more than fifty schools in Jefferson Parish, Louisiana, from elementary through high school, are taking part in WASTEBUSTERS. The program (Working Association of Students Tending to the Environment) includes drop-off centers at the schools for throwaways that can be recycled and also hands-on activities that promote understanding of environmental issues.

Recycling is a major environmental program in the Crippled Children's Hospital and School in Sioux Falls, South Dakota. After teacher Lee Anne Baldwin finished teaching an environmental unit, students in her special education class initiated Wheel Chair Recyclers, a program that won a United Nations award in 1991.

"Students noticed that a lot of paper in the school was being thrown away, so they decided they should find a way to pick it up. They presented their idea to the school's senior managers who helped adapt recycling barrels with wheels. Students in wheelchairs push the barrels around the school, collecting recyclable paper," Baldwin said,

In Connecticut, the Department of Environmental Protection sponsors programs by a recycling superhero. Ray Cycle™ goes to schools to emphasize with music and stories that individuals can take part in recycling as a way to care for the Earth.

adding, "They also are responsible for calling Northern Plains Recycling, the company that picks up the paper. Ordinarily, the company doesn't handle small amounts of paper, but because of the circumstances in this case they provided the service," she explained. Wheel Chair Recyclers also make posters and present information about the need for recycling to the rest of the school.[5]

In some schools, students go beyond collecting recyclable materials and become political activists. Consider the Students for a Better Environment club at suburban Willowbrook High School west of Chicago, Illinois. Club members developed and circulated a petition to remove plastic foam cups and trays from the school cafeteria. After receiving the petition, school administrators granted the request.

The club also publishes an environmental newsletter that is distributed to students and local lawmakers. Club members gather information about an issue and then try to develop awareness among students so that they will generate some type of action. Wendy Taylor, who was president of the club during the 1989–90 school year, said that club members enjoy learning and then turn around to become teachers themselves. "It's a process that really transforms the students from indifferent into active citizens," she said.[6]

Students at the Crippled Children's Hospital and School in Sioux Falls, South Dakota, launched Wheel Chair Recyclers, a recycling effort that won an international award in 1991.

Precycling and Reducing Waste

"To PRECYCLE is to make buying choices that support responsible products and packaging, make recycling easier and reduce the amount of garbage you throw away," states an Environmental Defense Fund (EDF) brochure. The Environmental Defense Fund is a national organization that focuses on federal policies regarding the environment and has had a long-time interest in solid-waste management.[7]

Precycling is one way that each of us can help reduce the amount of throwaways generated. Most precycling takes place at supermarkets because that is where the majority of Americans shop, particularly for packaged materials and disposable products.

Several organizations, including EDF, recommend precycling tips for supermarket shopping, such as buying durable mugs, glasses, or cups instead of throwaway containers for beverages, and avoiding products that are over-packaged—containers nestled in wrapping within boxes covered with a wrap.

One other way to be a wastebuster is to compost. Organic wastes—food scraps (except for meats and dairy foods that attract unwanted insects and animals), yard wastes, and other materials that were once alive—can be piled in a compost heap and allowed to rot. Worms added to the compost will help speed up the process of decomposition. The final product can be used as fertilizer.

School classes and student environmental clubs have experimented with compost heaps as a way to learn about the environment and the need for recycling. As young people observe that some materials biodegrade and others do not, they soon see the importance of reusing organic materials in compost and reducing other kinds of trash.

After taking part in such learning projects, students are likely to urge their parents to recycle and reduce waste at home. In fact, many parents of young children say they hear so much about recycling, composting, and other waste reduction methods that they are forced to take action.

"Kids just don't let up on you," one father said. "It's like the smoking thing. My kids bugged me about my habit until I quit. I'm finally getting the message about recycling, too. It's a matter of changing a bad habit—throwing everything away—and taking a few minutes to sort out the stuff for recycling and composting. That's much easier than to stop smoking!"[8]

A few cities have launched public educational programs to encourage residents to compost in their own backyards. One of the first and most successful is called the Backyard Compost Program. It began in 1985 in the city of Seattle, Washington. The city distributed 12,000 free compost bins to residents and taught volunteers the techniques of composting through a Master Composter program. Trained volunteers then taught others by taking their "garbage into gold" message out

WE CAN is a New York City recycling network that diverts 5,000 tons of solid waste from landfills each year. The program helps the poor and homeless who collect recyclable containers that can be returned to the center for deposits. More than $1 million is paid annually to those who redeem containers.

into their community, presenting slide shows, demonstration projects, classroom programs, and workshops. The program has been so successful that it is being adopted in other parts of the nation, such as in Washington, D.C., and Connecticut.[9]

Since 30 to 60 percent of the solid waste that goes to landfills can be composted, over a dozen U.S. cities have established compost programs as part of their solid waste management efforts. More than 150 compost programs are being planned. In such programs, solid waste is sorted to remove materials like glass, plastic, and metal, which cannot be composted. Food scraps, grass, leaves, and paper go through the composting process, which is similar to the natural breakdown of material, but more heat, water, and oxygen in the composting facility help the materials degrade faster.

In 1990 Procter & Gamble Company, manufacturers of many brand name products, committed $20 million to fund major projects that will encourage accelerated municipal composting. The company also announced that its Pampers and Luvs brands of disposable diapers would be "as fully compostable as possible." Procter & Gamble has often been asked about the possibility of developing a biodegradable diaper. But this would do little to solve the solid waste problem because diapers would not break down in landfills that are tightly compacted.

Eighty percent of a Procter & Gamble disposable diapers can be composted, and the company expects to develop a degradable material to replace the plastic back-sheet in diapers. A number of scientists working for environmental groups and in agricultural departments of universities have praised the company's efforts to encourage not only composting but also the use of compost to reclaim land, add nutrients to cropland, and prevent soil erosion.[10]

6
Fighting Toxins

One of the most difficult jobs for environmental caretakers is trying to prevent the menace of toxic waste and other hazardous materials in the environment, which include chemicals that can endanger human health. Many of these substances are deliberately dumped or accidentally released from industries or from toxic waste sites or incinerators that burn hazardous materials.

In the late 1970s, the general public became aware of the dangers of hazardous waste when problems surfaced at an abandoned canal, called Love Canal, in New York. Lois Marie Gibbs, a homemaker living nearby, learned that thousands of tons of toxic materials had been buried in the canal and covered over with dirt, a common waste-disposal practice during the 1950s and 1960s. But poisonous chemicals from the site seeped into groundwater and

This citizen group in East Liverpool, Ohio, is protesting the building of an incinerator to burn hazardous waste in their community. The grassroots group is one of over 7,600 that CCHW has helped organize and fight hazardous waste facilities near their homes.

bubbled to the surface, creating serious health problems for members of the Gibbs family and their neighbors.

Lois Gibbs led the way in bringing together a coalition of her neighbors, which eventually became known as the Citizens Clearinghouse for Hazardous Waste (CCHW). The organization called attention to the problems at Love Canal and with much effort was able to obtain government aid to relocate families away from the site. It has continued to help other grassroots groups across the nation organize to fight toxic wastes in their own backyards, and in 1990 Gibbs received one of the first Goldman prizes for her heroic leadership.

Community Workers

Following the example of the Love Canal organizers, citizens in Sumter County, Alabama, decided in the early 1980s that they would launch a campaign against a hazardous waste dump owned by ChemWaste. Known as the "Cadillac of Landfills," the waste site is the nation's largest and spreads across 2,700 acres of Sumter County. In 1989 the landfill accepted over 800,000 tons of hazardous waste—more than six times the volume taken in by the nation's next largest facility. Toxic waste came from 48 states and several countries.

The county government reportedly received $5 for every ton of waste brought to the landfill. But unemployment soared. Because of the landfill, local industries and businesses closed down. At least 1,700 residents moved away. Those who stayed fear for their health and lives because of fires, explosions, and leaks from the hazardous waste facility. They also fear another danger—Chem-Waste's plan to build a huge incinerator to burn hazardous waste, which could release dangerous substances into the environment.

How have citizens fought "city hall" and "big business"? The task has not been simple. Under the leadership of Kaye Kiker of York, Alabama, citizens organized a group called Alabamians for a Clean Environment (ACE), which included students and adults and sometimes entire families. Group members gathered information and took part in a variety of actions to call attention to the potential dangers of an incinerator as well as the landfill.

Kiker explained that ACE followed no special plan. "One time we chain ourselves to a gate, the next time we hold a community prayer," she reported.[1]

The group was able to pressure regulators to supervise the ChemWaste facility, and since 1983 the company has paid over $1 million in fines for repeatedly violating its permit, which allows only certain kinds of waste to be accepted. In addition, because of ACE and other group efforts, the Alabama legislature is attempting to set up the legal means to stop imports from states that do not make attempts to dispose of waste materials generated within their own borders. (Because of interstate commerce regulations, states cannot at present block imports of trash from other states.)

When students at El Puente, an alternative school in Brooklyn, New York, learned about a toxic waste site in their Hispanic community of Williamsburg, they also organized. Most people in the community had never been informed about the dump site, so the students were determined to spread the word about the dangers of toxic waste.

Calling themselves "Toxic Avengers," the students began their campaign in 1988 to stop expansion of the dump site and to prevent the construction of a hazardous waste incinerator nearby. Part of the Toxic Avengers' campaign is to fight "environmental racism." The term has been used by many environmentalists who are protesting the practice of placing hazardous facilities—whether toxic waste disposal sites or dangerous chemical industries—in neighborhoods and communities where residents are primarily people of color or are very poor. "It's as if governments and industries think Hispanics and other minority groups don't care about their neighborhood, but they do care," one of the Avengers said. "We want the toxic waste site out of here!" another spokesperson said.[2]

Many other community groups have attempted to keep hazardous waste out of their town or neighborhood or to stop the release of hazardous materials into the environment. The grassroots campaigns are varied and occur all across the United States. A group in California, for example, has been protesting a practice by a supermarket chain to spray insecticides on fresh fruits and vegetables. The purpose is to kill flies, gnats, and other flying insects. But if ingested, the insecticides also are poisonous to people.

Along the Gulf Coast in Louisiana, citizen groups have held a number of marches, chanting, "Clean it up, or shut it down!" They are demanding that a vast complex of chemical plants reduce the toxic emissions that pollute the air and have been linked to health problems among residents.

Citizen groups in many states pressure lawmakers to find ways and funds to clean up groundwater contaminated with pesticides, industrial wastes, or radioactive materials from nuclear power and weapons plants. Others fight to prevent the dumping of toxic materials in bays, rivers, and streams.

In many communities, businesses or volunteer groups set up facilities for recycling motor oil and used batteries, products that can contaminate land and water resources if dumped on the ground or into sewer drains. An increasing number of communities also conduct annual collections of hazardous household waste. Citizens can take dangerous throwaway items to a central location where workers sort and properly dispose of hazardous substances. What are dangerous throwaways? They include leftover household products such as drain cleaners, paint thinners and strippers, oven cleaners, deodorizers, degreasers, and bleaches.

Reducing Toxins at the Source

Although there is still a long way to go before safer materials and cleaner technology are commonplace in

Household products like these contain hazardous materials. Many communities conduct volunteer programs to collect leftover hazardous materials for safe disposal.

industrialized nations, reducing toxic pollutants at the source is the goal of an increasing number of U.S. industries. Companies have found that caring for the earth saves money that might be spent for pollution controls or levied in fines for contaminating the environment. Industries also save by reducing the use of raw materials.

There is another benefit to waste reduction. Companies gain a favorable reputation for being environmentally responsible. In fact, in Prospect Heights, Illinois, students, under adult supervision, have provided businesses with ideas for reducing waste and then awarded those that have improved their waste-generating habits. The effort has helped raise awareness of what it means to be a "good neighbor."

One U.S. firm that has pioneered in efforts to minimize toxic waste and prevent pollution is the 3M company in St. Paul, Minnesota. Although the company is at the top of the list in toxic emissions by U.S. industrial firms, 3M has been reducing pollutants every year since 1975 and plans to continue its efforts. Already 3M has cut emissions of pollutants into the air and land by hundreds of thousands of tons, reduced waste water by 1.6 billion gallons, and conserved vast amounts of energy, saving the company hundreds of millions of dollars.[3]

Procter & Gamble also has reduced waste at the source. Along with its programs to promote composting, the company uses recycled materials in its packaging for liquid laundry detergents, reuses food processing scraps to make animal feed, and in some plants has been able to recycle nearly all waste from manufacturing.

The well-known McDonald's Corporation has developed a plan to reduce waste by 80 percent at its thousands of restaurants worldwide. In 1990, McDonald's joined forces with the Environmental Defense Fund (EDF). The two organizations set up a task force that could work together rather than confront each other in protests or legal battles over such wastes as foam plastic packaging. Each organization paid its own expenses.

An EDF biochemist and waste management expert, Richard A. Denison, devised the plan, which includes more than forty projects and could be a model for waste reduction in other companies. One immediate action was to replace polystyrene (foam plastic) "clamshells" with thin paper wraps for sandwiches, reducing the volume of packaging materials by 70 to 90 percent. The company also switched to paper products that have not been bleached with chlorine, a chemical that pollutes water resources at paper mill sites. Other efforts include recycling materials whenever possible, buying recycled products, and replacing disposable containers with reusable ones for shipment of bulk supplies.

Wal-Mart, the nation's largest retailer, has set up recycling bins at each of its stores throughout the United States and uses recycled paper for its newspaper advertising inserts, circulars, and store signs and posters. The company also encourages individual stores to get involved with local

These wind machines in California are producing electricity. Researchers are trying to develop renewable energy resources such as wind and solar power. Renewable energy can help prevent air pollutants such as those that come from burning fossil fuels.

environmental programs, whether cleaning up a highway or stream or helping out with hazardous waste collection.

The Kroger chain of grocery stores has confronted the solid waste problem and initiated numerous activities to reduce waste and recycle materials. In 1990 the company estimates that it recycled more than 300 tons of office paper, 300,000 tons of corrugated paper, and 10 million pounds of old telephone directories. Kroger also has set up collection bins for recyclable aluminum, glass, and plastic. The company says that in 1990 some 411.5 million containers were collected, enough to fill 16,334 trailers that, lined up end-to-end, would stretch from Cincinnati to Indianapolis.[4]

Another major retailer, Target, has established environmental programs. Target officials say that because the company is a major developer and distributor of consumer goods, it has a responsibility to do its part to protect the environment, particularly in reducing solid waste and toxic materials. As part of this effort, the company supports Kids for Saving Earth, an international organization dedicated to helping kids become more involved in protecting the planet. Booklets and other materials on how to start Kids for Saving Earth clubs are available in Target stores. Many of these clubs are active in schools, and each year the company selects clubs to honor nationally and internationally for their creative and effective projects.

7
"Going Green" in the Marketplace

In telephone surveys during April 1991, the Gallup Organization found that well over half of the 1,007 Americans polled were greatly concerned about such problems as toxic waste, air and water pollution, the greenhouse effect, destruction of natural habitats for wildlife, and loss of tropical rain forests. Americans felt that business and industry were not concerned enough about the environment. Respondents believed that a tax or fee should be levied on corporations that manufacture environmentally harmful products or that produce hazardous waste and emissions during the manufacturing process. Most favored bans on chemicals such as chlorofluorocarbons (CFCs) even if that meant higher prices for products.

When asked what they personally had done in recent years to improve the quality of the environment, only 18 percent of those polled had volunteered to work for an

California cities are using alternative fuels, such as methanol, in public buses and other municipal vehicles to help reduce air pollution.

environmental group. But more than half had contributed funds. Nearly half cut down on the use of a car by taking public transportation or joining a car pool, but 67 percent of respondents or members of their households replaced a gas-guzzling car with one that used fuel more efficiently. More than 70 percent cut their household energy use, and 84 percent of the respondents or members of their families voluntarily recycled materials.[1]

If these poll results are any indication, many Americans appear to be "green" consumers. That is, their concerns for the environment determine how and what they will buy, what they will do about disposable items, and how they will conserve. But it is still very difficult for many people to put their environmental concerns into action. In many cases, consumers are not sure what to do or are not really aware that individuals can make a difference. Thus, a variety of print materials and TV programs are publicizing ways that consumers can take action.

Famous Environmental Activists

Many famous TV and film stars have been able to call attention to environmental problems and the way consumers can help solve them. Stars like Meryl Streep and Kevin Costner, for example, have been closely associated with the environmental movement.

Superstar Robert Redford has been an environmental activist since 1969 and has consistently pressured for energy conservation and use of solar power. Redford also has protected a mountain area in Utah by buying 5,000 acres there and establishing the Institute for Resource Management. The institute was set up to bring environmentalists together to discuss ways to cooperate in preserving both the environment and the economy.

Actor Ed Begley, Jr. is another long-time activist and green consumer. Begley gave up his gasoline-powered car and drives an electric car that he charges using solar panels on the roof of his garage. He also frequently travels by bicycle to Los Angeles from his home in the San Fernando Valley in California. He takes a collapsible bike with him when he uses public transportation, even when traveling cross-country.

Begley's choices for means of travel are not particularly convenient or easy, but he decided the alternative transportation was one way an individual could help reduce air pollutants and make a statement about environmental preservation. In Begley's words: "My methods may be extreme for many people, but I think we have to begin to do something about the environment in our personal lives. We can't wait all day for legislatures or corporations to act."[2]

Ted Turner, owner of the Turner Broadcasting System (TBS) and its Cable News Network (CNN), has called for "a cease-fire against the environment," making protection of the earth a personal crusade; TBS has been producing and airing numerous documentaries and other programs on environmental issues over its Cable News Network.

In 1980 Turner hired Barbara Y. E. Pyle to produce environmental programs that focused on critical global issues and were understandable and available to the widest possible audience. Since then, Pyle has won many awards for her film work and in 1989 became vice-president of environmental policy for TBS.

Among many duties, Pyle oversees news gathering on environmental issues worldwide, produces documentaries, and supervises the daily CNN news story called "Earth Matters." Pyle also co-directs *Captain Planet and the Planeteers*, an animated children's TV series about a super-hero and five children who travel the globe battling polluters and other enemies of the earth. The program airs on TBS and in nearly 200 different broadcasting stations nationwide and in more than eighty countries.

The philosophy behind environmental programming on TBS and its news network is best summed up by Pyle: "Our planet will not be saved by any one big decision, but by many individual choices made by people like you and me. Television has an important responsibility to provide us with the information necessary to enable us to make these choices."[3]

Making Choices

People who want to protect the planet and their own community, neighborhood, or backyard must make be-havior choices as well as choices about goods and services. For example, they may decide to be more conscientious

Putting groceries in a reusable canvas bag is a way to reduce waste and save natural resources.

about switching off lights when no one is in a room or conserving water or using nonpolluting sources of transportation. Some people may decide to reduce or eliminate their use of toxic chemical products for the home, garden, or yard. Others may decide to recycle, to reuse as many items as possible, or to buy green products when available.

Buying green products is not a simple matter, however, Consumers cannot always trust advertising claims about green goods and services. Are they really "environment-friendly," or are businesses and companies simply using the term to increase sales?

To answer that question, a number of organizations are acting as consumer watchdogs. One is the Council on Economic Priorities, which rates companies on their social and environmental citizenship. The council publishes its ratings in an annual paperback guide.

Consumer and environmental groups also publish information in their newsletters and magazines about green products and services and warn against products that carry misleading advertising. Newspapers and consumer magazines, including such diverse publications as *Changing Times, Garbage,* and *USA Weekend,* have carried articles on green supermarket shopping.

The EPA is trying to develop voluntary guidelines for environmental terms, as is a coalition of industry and trade groups. Some states have passed laws that govern how environmental terms can be used in advertising and on packaging. Two nonprofit organizations,

By reading labels, shoppers can determine whether a product is made from recycled materials or is in a container made from recycled paper or paperboard.

Green Cross Certification Company and Green Seal Incorporated, are beginning to issue seals of approval for U.S. products that have been analyzed and found to be safe for the environment. Other countries also issue approval labels for environment-friendly products. Those that have been in force the longest are in Germany and Canada. Japan, Norway, Sweden, and France are among the nations with green labeling programs under way.

When it comes to making personal buying decisions, shoppers have to decide whether they will really change their habits and purchase green products and services. Frequently this means paying a higher price. But if an increasing number of consumers demand goods and services that do not waste resources or harm the environment, the greater demand can bring prices down.

Finally, if YOU want to be a caretaker of the earth, you may already have some ideas on how to be an environment-friendly consumer. If you are wondering about other ways to be a protector of the planet, the What You Can Do and Where to Write sections may suggest some possibilities. If so, go for it! As one young person observed, "We all have to change our habits . . . it isn't like we have another planet to go to and live."[4]

What You Can Do

To Save Energy

- Turn off lights, TV sets, radios, and electrical appliances that are not being used.

- Use energy-efficient light bulbs.

- Keep doors and windows closed to prevent heat or cool air from escaping; encourage the use of insulating materials.

- Make fewer trips to the refrigerator and keep the door open only a few seconds.

- Run clothes washers only when full (but not overloaded).

- Walk, ride a bicycle, or use public transportation whenever possible.

To Conserve Water

- Install or ask someone in your household to install a water-saving shower head.

- Let the rain wash cars.

- Sweep sidewalks and outdoor porches when possible rather than hosing them down with water.

- Shut off running water while brushing your teeth.

- Put a water displacer in your toilet tank (a brick or plastic bottle weighted with stones will do).

To Protect the Land

- Learn to compost.

- Use organic pesticides and fertilizers.

- Encourage birds, frogs, and beneficial insects to inhabit your backyard or nearby vacant lot (many books and environmental magazines explain how).

- Dispose of oil, cleaners, and other toxic products in the proper way (*see* Chapter 6) rather than dumping them on land.

- Start or join a restoration or conservation project.

To Preserve Forests and Wildlife

- Avoid buying wood products made from tropical hardwoods.

- Eat less beef to reduce cattle grazing in the tropics.

- Forgo products that threaten endangered species, such as tortoise shell combs or items made from animal tusks.

- Support groups working to protect endangered animals and plant life.

To Prevent Air Pollution

- Plant trees.
- Avoid using aerosol sprays.
- Shred yard waste and mulch leaves for compost or take them to a municipal composting facility rather than burn them.

To Reduce Waste

- Refuse to buy items that cannot be reused, such as disposable plates, cups, and eating utensils.
- Buy reusable products or those in reusable containers or in containers that will be recycled.
- Use your own shopping bag. A canvas or string bag can be used over and over again and can save great amounts of plastic and paper.
- Find ways to refurbish old items.
- Share unwanted books, clothing, furniture, sports equipment, and other items with people in need.

To Learn about the Environment

- Visit environmental or nature centers, zoos and parks with wildlife programs, and marine educational facilities.

- Read about environmental issues such as acid rain, garbage disposal, the greenhouse effect, the ozone layer, air and water pollution, and toxic waste.

- Watch TV documentaries on the environment.

- Participate in environmental projects in your school or community.

To Be an Activist

- Start a recycling project.

- Join an environmental group or club that supports action projects.

- Talk to friends and family about the positive actions they can take to protect the planet.

- Write protest letters to companies that pollute and to government officials who do not take action to protect the environment.

- Send thank-you notes to company and government officials who act as caretakers of the earth.

Notes by Chapter

Chapter 1

1. Gaylord Nelson, "Earth Day, Then and Now: Reflections by Its Founder," *E Magazine* (March/April 1990), p. 58.

Chapter 2

1. Quoted in Elliot Diringer, "Environmental Prize for 6 'Grass-Root Heroes,'" *San Francisco Chronicle* (April 17, 1990), p. A4.

2. Dale Eisler, "Fields of a Dream," *Maclean's* (September 17, 1990), p. 47; Board on Agriculture of the National Research Council, *Alternative Agriculture* (Washington, D.C.: National Academy Press, 1989), pp. 8 and 23.

3. U.S. Environmental Protection Agency, *America's Wetlands: Our Vital Link Between Land and Water,* booklet, (Washington, D.C.: EPA Office of Wetlands Protection, February 1988), p. 6.

4. Quoted in Michael Weisskopf, "EPA's Reilly to Veto Dam," *The Washington Post* (November 23, 1990), p. A1; Jerry Adler with Karen Springen, "Where Will the Cranes Go?" *Newsweek* (April 3, 1989), pp. 62–63.

5. Diana Echevarria, phone interview and correspondence with author, August 1991.

6. David Seideman, "Wading Into the Fight," *National Wildlife* (December/January 1991), p. 36.

7. Andrew Holleman, phone interview with author, August 1991; Andrew Holleman, "David Meets Goliath in City Hall," *Mother Earth News (March/April 1990), pp. 48 and 50.*

Chapter 3

1. Kathie Durbin, "Northwest Forests: Day of Reckoning," *The Oregonian* (series of articles, September 18–21, 1991); "The Year of the Deal: 23rd Environmental Quality Index," *National Wildlife* (January/February 1991), p. 37; Karen Springen, "Old Allies in a Timber War," *Newsweek* (September 24, 1990), p. 31; Rowe Findley, "Old-Growth Forests: Will We Save Our Own?" *National Geographic* (September 1990), pp. 106–136.

2. "Scientists on a Hot Seat," *National Wildlife (December/January 1991), p. 28.*

3. Global Action Network, "Background Information for Tropical Forests," EcoNet electronic conference, February 6, 1991.

4. Chris Wille, "Buy or Boycott Tropical Hardwoods?" *American Forests* (July/August 1991), pp. 26 and 60.

5. "Saviors of the Planet," *Time* (April 29, 1991), p. 67.

Chapter 4

1. Center for Marine Conservation, "Global Efforts to Stop Marine Debris," *Coastal Connection* (Spring 1991), p. 1.

2. Center for Marine Conservation, "America's Beaches Still Awash with Trash," *Coastal Connection* (Summer 1990), p. 1.

3. "Dolphin Safe Canner Honored," Environment News Service, electronic newsline (May 10, 1991).

4. Trish Hall, "How Classroom Crusaders Saved the Dolphin from the Net," *The New York Times* (April 18, 1990), p. B1.

5. "History of GREEN," EcoNet electronic conference, July 1, 1991.

Chapter 5

1. "Hooked on Packaging," *Environmental Action* (March/April 1991), p. 25.

2. Thomas Kerr, "Groundswell of Interest Prompts Publication of Recycling Manual," *Chemecology* (February 1991), pp. 4–5; Lewis Beale, "Greener on the Other Side of the Border," Detroit Free Press (March 18, 1990), pp. 1H and 6H.

3. Karin Rettinger, "Cattle Farmers Find Use for Recycled Newspapers," *South Bend Tribune* (June 2, 1991), p. D1.

4. "Chapters Launch a Backlash Against Trash," *Modern Maturity* (April/May 1990), pp. 86–87.

5. Lee Anne Baldwin, phone interview with author, August 1991.

6. Quoted in Jody Temkin, "Teens Again Trying to Change the World," *Chicago Tribune* (January 28, 1990), Chicagoland section, p. 1.

7. "Precycling: How to Shop for Future Generations," *Recycling World* (1990), no page number.

8. Personal interview, April 1991.

9. Cindy Mitlo, "Master Composters Help Residents Turn Garbage Into Gold." *The Urban Ecologist* (Summer 1991), p. 3.

10. "P&G Commits $20 Million to Advance Composting as a Solid Waste Solution" (Proctor & Gamble news release, October 9, 1990).

Chapter 6

1. Quoted in The Environmental Exchange, "Our Backyard's Full," *Action Exchange* (undated bulletin).

2. The Toxic Avengers, phone interview with author, August 1991; Marguerite Holloway, "Get Out of Town," *Mother Jones* (April/May 1990), p. 17.

3. Jackey Gold, "The Pioneers," reprinted in *The Earth Care Annual 1991* (Emmanus, Pa.: Rodale Press), p. 124; Lois R. Ember, "Strategies for Reducing Pollution at the Source Are Gaining Ground," *Chemical & Engineering News* (July 8, 1991), p. 12.

4. "What Kroger is Doing About the Solid Waste Dilemma" (undated company flyer).

Chapter 7

1. Roper Center for Public Opinion Research, electronic data on Gallup Organization polls between April 11 and April 14, 1991.

2. Quoted in Connie Koenenn, "The Converts Go by Bus or Bike, on Skates or Foot," *Los Angeles Times* (June 19, 1990), p. E1.

3. TBS news release, May 1991, and author's telephone interview with Jessica Handler at CNN, July 1991.

4. Quoted in *Kids for Saving Earth Guidebook* (Plymouth, Minn.: Kids for Saving Earth, 1990), p. 16.

Glossary

biodegradable—the property of a substance that allows microorganisms to break it down into simple, stable compounds.

bioremediation—a process in which bacteria and fungi feed on various pollutants in water and soil.

CFCs—abbreviation for chlorofluorocarbons, which are gases used in refrigerators, air conditioners, and the making of plastic foam.

compost—plant and vegetable matter that have decayed and can be used as fertilizer.

carbon dioxide—an odorless, tasteless, and colorless gas that is part of air and is released when humans and other animals exhale or when substances containing carbon are burned.

ecology—the study of how living things relate to their environment.

ecosystem—a biological community; plants and animals that live together and depend on each other for survival.

endangered species—animals and plants in danger of becoming extinct (gone forever).

EPA—Environmental Protection Agency.

estuary—area of a river near the sea where fresh water and seawater mix.

fossil fuels—fuels such as oil and coal that come from decayed matter.

fungi (plural)—plant-like organisms; one of the classifications of living things.

global warming—an increase in global temperatures brought about by the accumulation of gases in the atmosphere.

habitat—living space for animals and plants; an area where there is food, water, and shelter for living organisms.

indigenous—living naturally in an area; native.

leach—to extract, such as to remove substances from soil as water seeps through.

organic (in agriculture and gardening)—refers to growing and raising plants and animals without the use of synthetic chemicals.

ozone layer—a layer of gas in the stratosphere that shields the earth from the ultraviolet rays of the sun.

polystyrene—foam plastic.

toxin—a poison.

tributary—a stream or river that flows into a larger waterway.

tropical rain forests—woodland areas in the tropics that receive at least 100 inches of rain each year.

watershed—a drainage basin; the area from which water drains into a water body such as a river or lake.

Where to Write

Center for Marine Conservation, 1725 DeSales St. NW, Suite 500, Washington, DC 20036

Citizen's Clearinghouse for Hazardous Wastes, P.O. Box 6806, Falls Church, VA 22040

Council on Economic Priorities, 30 Irving Place, New York, NY 10003

The Cousteau Society, 930 W. 21st St., Norfolk, VA 23517

Environmental Action Foundation, 1525 New Hampshire Ave. NW, Washington, DC 20036

Friends of the Earth, 218 D St. SE, Washington, DC 20003

Global ReLeaf program, American Forestry Association, P.O. Box 2000, Washington, DC 20013

Greenpeace USA, 1436 U St. NW, Washington, DC 20009

Household Products Disposal Council, 1201 Connecticut Ave. NW, Suite 300, Washington, DC 20036

Izaak Walton League of America, 1401 Wilson Blvd., Level B, Arlington, VA 22209

Keep America Beautiful, Inc., 9 W. Broad St., Stamford, CT 06902

Kids for Saving Earth, P.O. Box 47247, Plymouth, MN 55447

National Arbor Day Foundation, 100 Arbor Ave., Nebraska City, NB 68410

National Audubon Society, 950 Third Ave., New York, NY 10022

National Wildlife Federation, 1400 16th St. NW, Washington, DC 20036-2266

Natural Resources Defense Council, 40 E. 20th St., New York, NY 10011

The Nature Conservancy, 1800 N. Kent St., Suite 800, Arlington, VA 22209

Pesticides Action Network—North America Regional Center, 965 Mission St., #514, San Francisco, CA 94103

Rainforest Action Network, 301 Broadway, Suite A, San Francisco, CA 94133

Sierra Club, 730 Polk St., San Francisco, CA 94109

U.S. Environmental Protection Agency, 401 M St. SW, Washington, DC 20460

The Wilderness Society, 900 17th St. NW, Washington, DC 20006

World Wildlife Fund, 1250 24th St. NW, Washington, DC 20037

Further Reading

Books and Booklets

Bullard, Robert D. *Dumping in Dixie: Race, Class and Environmental Quality.* Boulder, Colo.: Westview Press, 1990.

Council on Economic Priorities. *Shopping for a Better World.* New York: Council on Economic Priorities, 1991.

Crampton, Norm. *Complete Trash: The Best Way to Get Rid of Practically Everything Around the House.* New York: M. Evans, 1989.

Dadd, Debra Lynn. *The Nontoxic Home.* Los Angeles: Tarcher, 1986.

Earthworks Group. *50 Simple Things You Can Do to Save the Earth.* Berkeley, Calif.: Earthworks Press, 1990.

Elkington, John, Julia Hailes, and Joel Makower. *The Green Consumer.* New York: Viking Penguin, 1990.

Environmental Protection Agency. *Toxics in the Community.* Washington, D.C.: EPA, 1990.

Gay, Kathlyn. *Cleaning Nature Naturally.* New York: Walker, 1991.

———. *Garbage and Recycling.* Hillside, N.J.: Enslow, 1991.

Heloise. *Hints for a Healthy Planet.* New York: Perigee, 1990.

Kenworth, Lauren, and Eric Schaefer. *A Citizen's Guide to Promoting Toxic Waste Reduction.* New York: INFORM, 1990.

Kids for Saving Earth. *Kids for Saving Earth Guidebook*. Plymouth, Minn.: Clinton Hill's Kids for Saving Earth, 1990.

National Toxics Campaign. *Fighting Toxics*. Washington, D.C.: Island Press, 1990.

O'Hara, Kathryn J., Suzanne Iudicello, and Rose Bierce. *A Citizens Guide to Plastics in the Ocean: More Than a Litter Problem*. Washington, D.C.: Center for Environmental Education, 1988.

Pringle, Laurence. *Restoring Our Earth*. Hillside, N.J.: Enslow, 1987.

————. *Throwing Things Away: From Middens to Resource Recovery*. New York: Crowell, 1986.

Rifkin, Jeremy, ed. *The Green Lifestyle Handbook*. New York: Henry Holt, 1990.

Seager, Joni, ed. *The State of the Earth Atlas*. New York and London: Simon & Schuster, 1990.

Steger, Will, and Bowermaster, Jon. *Saving the Earth: A Citizen's Guide to Environmental Action*. New York: Knopf, 1990.

Wild, Russell, ed. *The Earth Care Annual 1992*. Emmaus, Pa.: Rodale, 1992. (Annuals also published in 1990 and 1991.)

Articles in Periodicals

Begley, Sharon. "Pollution Knows No Boundaries." *National Wildlife*, February/March 1990, pp. 34–43.

Brown, Lester, Christopher Flavin, and Sandra Postel. "A Global Plan to Save Our Planet's Environment." *USA Today* (magazine), January 1990, pp. 28–31.

"Canada's Green Plan: Blueprint for a Healthy Environment."
Environment, May 1991, pp. 14–20, 38–45.

Carroll, Ginny. "Green For Sale." *National Wildlife,*
January/February 1991, pp. 24–27.

"Citizen Crusaders" (five profiles). *Maclean's,* September 17,
1990, pp. 46–49.

Cohn, Roger. "Calabaza Pumpkins Are Growing in the Bronx!"
Audubon, July/August 1991, pp. 77–89.

"Do Good Things Come in Green Packages?" *Garbage,*
July–August 1990, p. 80.

"Earth Day: Who Cares?" *Newsweek,* April 16, 1990, p. 6.

Flattau, Edward. "Measuring the Pulse of the Earth." *E
Magazine,* November/December 1990, pp. 13–14, 66–69.

Gilbert, Bil. "Earth Day Plus 20, and Counting." *Smithsonian,*
April 1990, pp. 47–80.

"Green Revolution, The" *Advertising Age,* January 29, 1991,
entire issue.

Grossman, Dan, and Seth Shulman. "Down in the Dumps."
Discover, April 1990, pp. 36–41.

Hedstrom, Elizabeth. "Earth Day." *National Parks,* March/April
1990, pp. 18–23.

Hof, Robert D. "The Tiniest Toxic Avengers." *Business Week,*
June 4, 1990, pp. 96–98.

Holing, Dwight. "Looking for Mr. Goodbug." *Sierra,*
January/February 1990, pp. 20–24.

Kourik, Robert. "Controlling Pests Without Chemical
Warfare." *Garbage,* March/April 1990, pp. 22–29.

McDermott, Jeanne. "Some Heartland Farmers Just Say No to Chemicals." *Smithsonian,* April 1990, pp. 114–127.

Nichols, Mark. "The Green Generation." *Maclean's,* September 17, 1990, pp. 90–91.

Nixon, Will. "1990 Year of the Environment." *E Magazine,* January/February 1991, pp. 31–37.

Reiger, George. "Conservation Realities in the '90s." *American Forests,* March/April 1990, pp. 17–19.

Russell, Dick. "Environmental Movers & Shakers." *American Forests,* March/April 1990, pp. 24–27 and 76–77.

"Saviors of the Planet." *Time,* April 29, 1991, pp. 66–67.

Schneider, Paul. "Other People's Trash." *Audubon,* July/August 1991, pp. 108–119.

Silver, Marc. "Doing Your Bit to Save the Earth." *U.S. News & World Report,* April 2, 1990, pp. 61–63.

Springen, Karen, and Annetta Miller. "Doing the Right Thing." *Newsweek,* January 7, 1991, pp. 42–43.

Wang, Penelope. "It's Not Easy Being Green." *Money,* April 1990, pp. 101–112.

Waxman, Don. "Teaching Restoration to Kids." *Whole Earth Review,* Spring 1990, pp. 64–66.

Wolfson, Elissa. "Greening the Golden Arches?" *E Magazine,* November/December 1990, pp. 16–17.

———. "Uniting Nations for the Environment." *E Magazine,* July/August 1991, pp. 13–, 60–62.

INDEX